781.6 N714s

1939

ENTERED AUG 4 1999

PUBLISHED IN
CONJUNCTION WITH

**FROM THE
1939 WORLD'S FAIR**

PRODUCED BY EOS MUSIC INC.
ALICE TULLY HALL
LINCOLN CENTER
2 FEBRUARY 1998

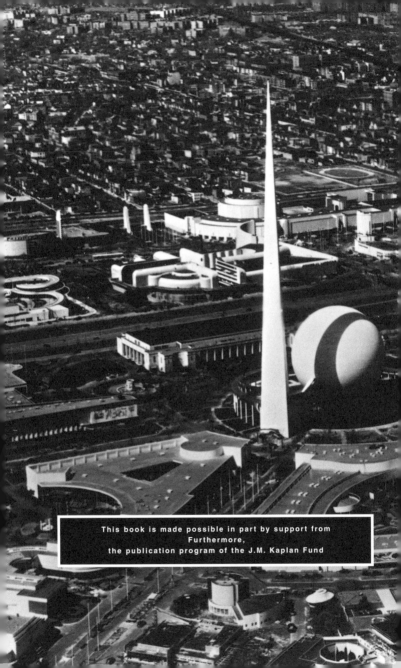

This book is made possible in part by support from
Furthermore,
the publication program of the J.M. Kaplan Fund

1 9 3 9

MUSIC
&
THE
WORLD'S
FAIR

Edited
by
Claudia SWAN

COLUMBIA COLLEGE LIBRARY
600 S. MICHIGAN AVENUE
CHICAGO IL 60605

Eos Music Inc.

Jonathan
SHEFFER
Artistic Director

781.6 N714s

1939

©1998
EOS Music Inc.
All rights reserved
Published by
Eos Music Inc., NY

Designed by Bureau, NY
Printed by Studley Press

ISBN 0-9648083-2-3

TABLE OF CONTENTS

DISCARD

F O R E W O R D

Jonathan SHEFFER

IN THIS THIRD EOS MUSIC FESTIVAL, WE
EXAMINE A SPECIFIC EVENT AS A POINT OF HISTOR-
ICAL PERSPECTIVE IN AMERICAN MUSIC. A study of
the World's Fair of 1939 offers many insights into the
state of the world in general and American culture in
particular at a critical fulcrum in the "American" century, at a moment when a transforming war would irrevo-
cably alter the political and cultural landscape. Like the
earlier expositions in Paris, St. Louis, and Chicago, the
1939 World's Fair seems, in retrospect, a relic of the
style of the times, a quaint barometer of the past's vision
of its own future. "The World of Tomorrow," the Fair's
theme, presented an imagined future (a short-range
view) that has already been surpassed as we approach
the end of the century.

    With hindsight, every expression of a given
time, from World's Fairs to Broadway musicals, from
Weimar cabaret songs to Futurist art, seems, ironically,
to speak about its own present so eloquently that the
inability to imagine a changed future strikes us as naive-
ly or dangerously jejune. But, of course, no populist art
ever became popular by peddling a pessimistic future: at
the bleakest time of the Depression, life was just a bowl
of cherries (which makes the success of "Brother Can
You Spare A Dime?" even more extraordinary). The Fair
of 1939 was entirely caught up in extolling the glories of
democracy, the utter success of consumerism (after an
unfortunate ten-year lapse) and the giddy possibilities of
a mechanized and technologically streamlined life avail-

able to everyone. The path between the twin threats of the lingering Depression and the coming cataclysm seems now to have been one of continued avoidance, of manufactured optimism. And the innocent, cheerful message, sung at every stop along a tour of the Fair, of a world (as rhymed by Ira Gershwin for the Fair's theme) "Where all creeds and races / Meet with smiling faces" put a cheerful spin on a complicated, untidy world.

In all respects, 1939 remains one of the most laden moments in our history – the year of the Hitler-Stalin Pact and the invasion of Poland, which swept Europe into war. So much political change occurred, in fact, that the Fair reopened in the spring of 1940 with a quite different complement of buildings from abroad: the Russian pavilion, and the pavilions of every country occupied by Germany during the first winter of war, were replaced or reconceived as lighter, less controversial fare. Ironically, in a climate of growing international anxiety, it was perhaps the year of Hollywood's greatest glory: *Citizen Kane, Gone with the Wind* and *The Wizard of Oz* all opened as the Fair greeted its first visitors.

The Fair called forth works of a wide variety, all dedicated to selling a determinedly positive view of the potential of science and industry to bring us a brighter future, and a daily existence made cleaner, healthier, and more efficient – in other words, improved comfort for mankind, the endlessly unfulfilled wish of history's planners. To these ends, the Fair's planners commissioned architects we now acknowledge to be the modernist masters, and insisted that the exhibit halls have no windows of any kind, which gave the entire campus a sleek, futuristic look. Similarly, painters and sculptors filled the halls and grounds with WPA-style depictions of everything from the history of medicine (in massive murals) to entwined lovers and solitary dreamers (in monumental sculptures) and other agents of human industry. Films and live shows needed music to promote their messages. Kay Swift, a dynamic Broadway and Hollywood arranger and composer, was hired to oversee the work of the late George Gershwin, Aaron Copland, Kurt Weill, Hans Eisler, George Antheil, Robert Russell Bennett, Oscar Levant and Arthur Schwartz, among many others. The resulting outpouring of occasional music was part of a healthy, growing American musical culture. 1939 saw the premiere of that most American of works, Roy Harris's epic Third Symphony.

In the same year, Leonard Bernstein graduated from Harvard, where he wrote his honors thesis on the racial characteristics of American music. While it is convenient to think of the Civil Rights struggle of the 1960s, and even the O. J. Simpson trial, as later, key events in the history of racial conflict in America, study of the Fair occupied an important — albeit quieter — position on the continuum of race relations. William Grant Still, a figure who could be likened to the Jackie Robinson of American concert music, was chosen in a (color)blind competition to compose a piece for the "Democracity" exhibit, which played continually inside the giant Perisphere, at the fair's Theme Center. Visitors to the exhibit stood on massive ringed balconies, over-looking a giant model of a futuristic city; Still's "Rising Tide" resounded in the background. A short, terribly earnest essay appeared inside the sheet music of Still's World's Fair song, describing it as "unique, unlike any-thing Still has ever written before, for its idiom is more or less universal: Containing two memorably written melodies, there is nothing Negroid about it." It went on to say that "He is far from exemplifying the popular con-ception of a Negro composer, and one cannot avoid mentioning the people who have been told that all colored people are imitators and who therefore search Still's music diligently for some evidence of imitation."

Aaron Copland, who worked hard at finding a self-consciously "American" style for concert music, also contributed to the Fair effort, and in very telling ways. His soundtrack for the documentary film *The City* gives full voice to both his chosen simplicity for an imagined rural American music (which would flower four years later in *Appalachian Spring*), as well as a spirited, driving evocation of our industrial, urban landscape. The film, with scenario by the leftist producer Pare Lorentz, extols social engineering in utopian cities as the cure for the ills of industrial society. Copland also composed music for a puppet show at the Hall of Pharmacy, entitled *From Sorcery to Science*, which was essentially a big infomercial for drug companies. This charming and evocative score (housed until now in the Library of Congress) contains some wonderful "lost" examples of his unique style: the pentatonic Oriental evocations (which always sound thoroughly American in their modernity), and diatonic parallel harmonies, used here in a sentimental, yet somehow muscular march. The text for this show, by an unknown author and read by Lowell Thomas in the best newsreel fashion, speaks of tribal medicine in no uncertain terms: "These unfortunate people never heard of anything but the beating of drums, superstition, and magic. Voodoo! These savages are to be pitied, because they live now when other people can enjoy all the benefits of modern science...." In both of these works, inspirational political speech of the times seems unbearably haughty by current standards.

We reflect here upon a period and an event that called forth strong responses from its citizens and its artists, in a way that seems totally alien to a world anaesthetized by information. If these works strike the listener as less than profound, if their clamor for the moral or commercial high ground tends to diminish them, we may still marvel at the passion that produced them, and the skill that pervades them and gives them some dazzle, however (like the Fair itself) transitory.

v

ART AT THE NEW YORK WORLD'S FAIR: A PERSONAL RETROSPECTIVE

Robert ROSENBLUM

FOR ME, THE NEW YORK WORLD'S FAIR OF 1939-40 IS A MAGICAL MIXTURE OF PRIVATE AND PUBLIC HISTORY. As a child who grew up in the Manhattan of the 1930s, I was bursting with anticipation of the long-promised arrival, on April 30, 1939, of what was heralded as the "World of Tomorrow" or, less commonly, as the "Dawn of a New Day" – the name of the Fair's theme song, written by Ira and George Gershwin. As soon as the school term was over, I rushed out to Flushing Meadow one summer day after another, to immerse myself in the Utopian universe the Fair promised to me and every other visitor. That it in fact turned out to be the very eve of Britain and France's official declaration of war on Germany was a chilling irony lost on me. I was eleven, going on twelve, and Europe and the Second World War seemed as distant as Pluto, whereas the Fair was just a short subway ride from Times Square. And once there, looking toward my own future together with the future the Fair guaranteed to the whole planet, I felt suspended between a past epoch and a new one, a dreamlike environment in which I could actually live and breathe for the better part of the summer months.

My own professional future turned out to be that of an art historian with traditional academic training and a particular interest in modern art. As such, I am often obliged to revisit with presumed objectivity the art and architecture of the 1930s and '40s, and to judge which stars were rising and which were falling, which artistic winds were blowing toward the future and which were already short of breath. And quickly moving from the objective domain of historical data to the subjective depths of childhood memory, I can now recall the Fair as something pivotal in the history of art, not only as I knew it firsthand from the New York of the late 1930s, but as something I might attempt to reconstruct with the decades of knowledge accrued since then.

I remember, as does everyone who was there, the cosmic geometries at the very core of the Fair – the Trylon and Perisphere, designed by Wallace K. Harrison and J. André Fouilhoux – sublime distillations of complementary eternal forms, the pyramid and the sphere, that could evoke everything from obelisks and planets to male and female symbols. And at night, when these sky-bound monuments were bathed in a bluish-purple light, their floating volumes of what looked like astronomic dimensions seemed to soar, weightlessly. I dimly recalled seeing such visions depicted in oil on canvas: and now, decades later, I realize that the celestial Trylon and Perisphere were in no small way the tangible realization of a trend in geometric paintings categorized as "Transcendental Abstraction." An almost occult form of spiritual quest that might be realized through the language of immaterial geometry, this strange art was the primary program of the Guggenheim Foundation's Museum of Non-Objective Painting, whose mystical quarters at 24 East 54 Street I had occasionally visited on my childhood rounds of New York's then free art museums. Today, I am delighted to discover that one of the major disciples of Wassily Kandinsky, Rudolf Bauer, whose works were abundantly collected by the Baroness Hilla Rebay, had invented, along with his other ruler-and-compass fantasies, the very image of the Trylon and Perisphere in a painting of 1936, loftily titled *The Holy One*. I am almost positive I saw it in the late 1930s, a blueprint on a museum wall that would soon become an awesome, spine-tingling reality. Today, such a connection between the ethereal aspirations of many practitioners of abstract painting and the symbolic geometries of the Fair's thematic core makes perfect sense as cultural history. Did it not introduce the poignant motif of a desperate, heaven-bound escape from the grim local and international realities of life on both sides of the Atlantic during the darkening decade of the 1930s? And of course, the historian can look farther backwards as well as forwards from the Trylon and Perisphere, remembering the largely unexecuted Utopian schemes of such late eighteenth-century French architects as Claude-Nicolas Ledoux and Étienne-Louis Boullée for ideal buildings of cosmic scale in the shape of pure spheres, pyramids, and cubes, or noting how in later fairs and theme parks, from the New York World's Fair of 1964-65 to EPCOT at Disney World, the central motif of a giant sphere that would carry us beyond Planet Earth would recur, though never again, in my view, with the absolute purity and innocent confidence of its appearance in 1939.

I recall, too, a far less conspicuous but, for me, equally unforgettable architectural moment at the Fair, the interior of the Finland Pavilion, designed by Alvar Aalto. Raised in the shadow of New York Art Deco buildings (I particularly loved Central Park West's pair of new two-towered apartment houses by Irwin Chanin, The Majestic and The Century), I had a childish preconception that the unyielding language of parallels and perpendiculars, streamlined ornament, and unframed corner windows was the only vehicle that could transport me to future happiness. What a shock, then, it was to walk into Aalto's modest building and be enclosed in what looked like the very opposite of a Machine Age Utopia, a womb-like space that evoked the remote density of some Nordic forest, with steeply tilted wooden walls undulating like wind and water.

This startling regression to the irrational shapes of nature offered an unexpected alternative to the straight line and the right angle; and throughout the Fair, I think I began to feel the subliminal rumblings of this rebellion against the pure geometries that for me, a child of the 1930s, had always been symbolic of the bounty of an ever more technological "World of Tomorrow."

Such throbbings, I realized, seemed to be struggling for freedom all over the Fair, perhaps most conspicuously in the fabulous loops of the ramp that wafted visitors up to General Motors' sensational Futurama. This chairbound voyage into centuries to come followed an equally irregular circuit that defied the Fair's axial planning. But being attuned to painting, thanks to precocious visits not only to the Museum of Non-Objective Painting, but to the equally new Museum of Modern Art and the Gallery of Living Art at New York University as well, I was attracted to these symptoms of change that were evident everywhere in the many large murals executed for the Fair by some now very famous artists. A vast indoor mural in the Aviation Building by Arshile Gorky represented the theme of Man's Conquest of the Air (a Brave New World motif he had already explored in his 1935-37 murals for the Newark Airport); and there, too, within a language that conjured up the precision of an engineer's draftsmanship, one would see an occasional hard-edged shape whose contours unexpectedly throbbed with the pulse of organic life. Such mixed messages were found in Ilya Bolotowsky's mural for the Hall of Medical Science as well. A disciple of Mondrian, Bolotowsky could nevertheless relax his parallel and perpendicular geometries enough to permit strangely animated intruders into his pristine fields: warped triangles, boomerangs, amoeboid templates. Much later I learned that Aalto's contribution to the Finland Pavilion, which seemed to be the spearhead of nature's rebellion against the machine, was in fact designed only as an interior that had to be contained within a pre-existing, modular convention hall of cubic volume. There, in a nutshell, Aalto had created a dialogue between those warring forces that were repeated throughout the Fair's painted murals.

This tug-of-war could also be seen in a mural at the Hall of Pharmacy by a great artist I had certainly never heard of in 1939, Willem de Kooning. Painted on a curving, trapezoidal ground that already spiraled away from rectilinear order, the mural, if hardly one of the artist's finest moments, gave further evidence of this see-sawing between the structure of rigorous geometry and the rebellion of more fluent, animated contours that, when fully realized, would wreak havoc on traditional law and order. Seismographically speaking, it was the marks registered by these tremors that made the deepest impression on me then and that now, seen in retrospect, carried the real future with them. Appropriately, an exhibition of art and design from these years to be held at the Brooklyn Museum in 1999 is titled "Vital Forms in American Art, 1941-62." It was the preview of this vitality that captured my young eyes.

This nascent force was to be found, too, in what I recall as the jazziest of the Fair's huge murals, Stuart Davis's *History of Communications*. With its bobbing fragments of everything from newspapers, telephones, and air-mail letters to human ears and mouths, the whole evoked the grandiose theme contained within the Hall of Communications. Executed in black and white, it snapped, crackled, and popped with energy from top to bottom and side to side. Decades later, it would become for me another art-historical landmark, much like Aalto's interior. Looking back with 20/20 hindsight at Davis's mural, could it have been a preview not only of the black-and-white *perpetuum mobile* compositions of such Abstract

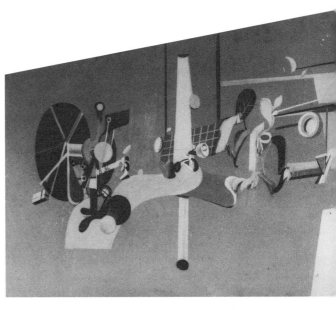

Expressionists as de Kooning and Jackson Pollock, but even of the hyperactive graffiti style of Keith Haring's public murals?

Of course, it is exactly this fusion of childhood recall and the accumulated knowledge of a professional art historian that gives the New York World's Fair a special aura for me. Already a convert to modern art, I looked at the monumental sculptural allegory of a star-holding worker that towered over the Soviet Union Pavilion and immediately dismissed it as bad art. These days, however, we have rediscovered the world of totalitarian art, now safely remote, and can even enjoy these bloated symbols as fascinating artifacts of a pathological

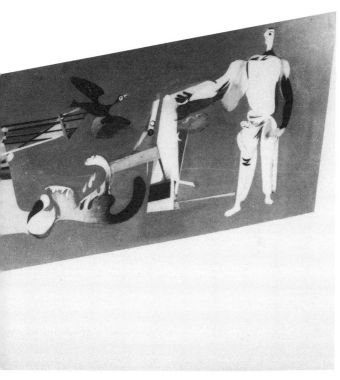

era. I remember, too, being awed by such Gulliverian fantasies as the National Cash Register Building, a nondescript cylinder that provided the base for a gigantic cash register, of science-fictional dimensions, that would ring up the staggering number of visitors to the Fair. And now, almost six decades later, my art historian's mind wants to see this as a preview of, say, Claes Oldenburg's giddy projects to make sky-high public monuments from the most ordinary things, whether electric fans or clothespins. I suspect that my sojourn in Flushing Meadow in 1939 will always remain for me a mysterious mixture of personal memory and the story of our century.

COPLAND
AT THE FAIR

Howard POLLACK

DURING THE SUMMER OF 1937, EN ROUTE FROM NEW YORK TO MEXICO, AARON COPLAND SPENT THE MONTH OF JUNE IN HOLLYWOOD IN THE HOPES OF LANDING A MOVIE CONTRACT. He wanted to partake in a medium that reached so many people (his motivation, too, for writing for radio and eventually television). Besides, he needed the cash. He was further encouraged by Hollywood's apparent receptivity to formally educated composers, not just those, like Max Steiner, who had come up through the ranks. Ernst Toch had composed a film score in 1935, as had Erich Wolfgang Korngold and Werner Janssen in 1936. Rumor had it that Paramount was negotiating with Shostakovich and had already engaged Schoenberg and Stravinsky. "It is just a matter of finding a feature film that needs my kind of music," Copland confidently wrote the Mexican composer, Carlos Chávez, before leaving New York.[1]

Copland met with Paramount music head Boros Morros, but nothing materialized. His growing following on the East Coast counted for naught in Hollywood. If anything, his reputation as a New York modernist (perhaps colored by memories of the boos and hisses that greeted his Piano Concerto at the Hollywood Bowl in 1928) made studio executives wary. Even in the wake of acclaim for his film score to *Of Mice and Men* (1939), producer Sol Lesser felt queasy about hiring such a musical radical for *Our Town* (1940) — as quaint as such reservations might strike us today. (As late as 1944, one critic would describe the *Lincoln Portrait* as "such as we have come to expect from the composer—angular, dissonant, and, as a setting for Lincoln's noble words, anachronistic.")[2] In any case, without a successful film credit, Copland was a nobody.

Copland returned to New York and in 1938 composed a ballet, *Billy the Kid*, for Lincoln Kirstein's Ballet Caravan; an orchestral piece, *An Outdoor Overture*, for the New York High School for the Performing Arts; a chorus, *Lark*, for the Dessoff Choir; and a setting of a Jewish-Palestinian folk song, "We've Come" ("Banu"). "It is not a time for poignantly subjective lieder," he explained, "but a time for large mass choral singing. It is the composer who must embody new communal ideals in a new communal music."[3] Although Copland's communist leanings peaked at about this time, they affected his life and career as a whole. He was by temperament a team player—from his teenage years when he assumed leadership roles at summer camp and when he joined other young volunteers harvesting berries in upstate New York on behalf of the boys fighting overseas. He achieved artistic maturity in a milieu—Paris in the early 1920s—in which collaboration had become a way of life. On his return to the States, he spearheaded concert series, launched careers, wrote for magazines and newspapers, headed organizations, co-founded a music press, toured foreign countries as cultural ambassador, joined various faculties, and conducted orchestras, all the while working intimately with musicians, composers, dancers, photographers, and actors. He was the antithesis of the hermetic composer who writes music in isolation for the delectation of future generations (though he periodically expressed himself more intimately, especially in his solo piano pieces).

Such collaborative ventures offered numerous incentives. On a practical level, they helped get his music played and advance his ever fragile and tenuous profession as a whole. Moreover, they had—especially in the 1930s and 1940s — social and political implications, in relation to the fight against fascism and European cultural domination, the advancement of democracy, and the education of young minds. In addition, he thrived on contact with other artists, both in and out of music. Whether writing a ballet for Martha Graham or a concerto for Benny Goodman, the very act of collaboration stimulated him. What these lofty collaborations generally did not offer was much in the way of financial remuneration. At least they paid something — not an inconsequential matter for a composer who in 1938 could not afford to travel up to Boston to hear the Boston Symphony perform his *El Salón México* (in the end, the conductor Serge Koussevitzky put him up in his own home). But they paid precious little: $150 for a ballet (1934) for Ruth Page and a mere $100 for an opera (1937) for the Henry Street Settlement. Only Hollywood was flush — and he had yet to find work there.

In early 1939 Copland composed incidental scores for two ill-fated Broadway productions: *Five Kings* and *Quiet City*. Jointly produced by the Theatre Guild and John Houseman's Mercury Theatre, *Five Kings* — written and directed by its star, Orson Welles — was a massive five-hour compilation of Shakespearean histories, with Burgess Meredith playing Prince Hal to Welles's Falstaff. Welles had worked with Copland before, directing the composer's Brechtian opera for adolescents, *The Second Hurricane* (1937) a few years earlier. For this grandiose undertaking, Copland duly provided a somewhat uncharacteristic score, drawing on English and French folksong, European sacred music, and even Lully in order to provide (not necessarily historically correct) period flavor. During out-of-town tryouts, the production ran into numerous problems, including climbing debt and malfunctioning equipment, and closed before its scheduled New York premiere.

Copland at least earned $1000 for the effort – an unusually large fee which helps explain why he accepted the commission in the first place. By contrast, he probably undertook to compose the score to Irwin Shaw's *Quiet City* with the promise of nothing more than royalties. Produced and directed by the founder of the Group Theatre and one of Copland's closest friends, Harold Clurman, the production had run into money problems. As someone very involved with the Group since its inception, Copland read the play and, intrigued by Shaw's drama of a middle-aged assimilated Jewish businessman in crisis, resolved to help his friends by providing the music himself. Unfortunately, the show flopped, although Copland's music, arranged as a suite the following year, survived the occasion to become one of his most beloved pieces.

With the opening of the New York World's Fair that same year came two more commissions: recorded scores for a puppet show, *From Sorcery to Science*, and for a documentary film, *The City*. Both played daily for the duration of the Fair at the Hall of Pharmacy and the Little Theatre of the Science and Education Building, respectively.

From Sorcery to Science commemorated the history of pharmacy from ancient China to modern times in short vignettes remembered by Copland as including "a Chinese medicine man, an old witch with a head seven feet long and an eye that lit up and popped, a hawk-faced medieval alchemist, an African witch doctor, two modern scientists, a modern druggist, and a modern beautiful girl."[4] It featured twelve-foot-high puppets designed by the celebrated Remo Bufano, who had earlier created puppets for productions of Falla's *El Retablo* and Stravinsky's *Oedipus Rex* mounted by New York's foremost guild of composers, the League of Composers. Such associations help account for this particular collaboration, for Copland was an active and prominent League member. In addition, the commission paid $850, a handsome fee for a piece that took him less than a week to write and, with the assistance of a young protégé, Henry Brant, orchestrate. The music was recorded with narration by the celebrated radio commentator, Lowell Thomas [see John Bell, "*From Sorcery to Science*," in this volume].

Copland's ten-minute score for a rather large orchestra containing two pianos and an exotic percussion battery (including temple blocks, claves, sleigh bells, and sandpaper) features pentatonic melodies for the Chinese medicine shop, accented tritones and chromatic burblings for the witch, modal harmonies and mysterious dissonances for the alchemist, conga-like syncopations for the "voodoo" witch doctor, noble triads for the contemporary scientists, and a spirited, tuneful march for the modern pharmacist. And yet Copland casts such hackneyed associations in a new light. The witch doctor episode, a wonderfully festive interlude reminiscent of Chávez, is particularly fetching; Copland would not essay so unrestrained an outburst for brass and percussion again until *Dance Panels* (1959). Also noteworthy is the ultradiatonic final march, which does not use a single accidental. Copland later thought he might recycle some of the score, in particular the concluding march, as a work for a band. He eventually gave up on that idea, but not before sketching some new music that subsequently served as the opening of *Rodeo* (1942). In 1941 the manuscript to *From Sorcery* was lost in the same theft that cost him two completed movements of the Piano Sonata, thus thwarting any other plans to reuse the music. Eventually, however, a detailed sketch score turned up at the New York Public Library and orchestral parts at the Library of Congress, allowing Wayne Shirley to reconstruct and edit a full score in 1996.[5]

Sponsored by the Carnegie Corporation at a cost of $50,000, the forty-five-minute *The City* was a high-profile, high-tone affair. Based on an idea by Pare Lorentz, it featured direction and cinematography by filmmaker-photographers Ralph Steiner and Willard Van Dyke, a scenario by Henwar Rodakiewicz, commentary by city planner Lewis Mumford narrated by Morris Carnovsky, and music by Copland; all accomplished, serious artists and thinkers. Both Steiner and Van Dyke had had a hand in the Pare Lorentz documentaries scored by Virgil Thomson: *The Plow that Broke the Plains* (1936) and *The River* (1937). Now they were collaborating on their own. *The City* premiered with considerable fanfare on 26 May 1939. It quickly established itself as a classic of its kind, probably the most celebrated of all of Van Dyke's distinguished documentaries.

    The City embodied some of the ideals and attitudes characteristic of that New York intelligentsia of which Copland was the dominant musical figure. All of the collaborators were communist sympathizers; all had had some relation to the photographer Alfred Stieglitz as well. Copland had been especially close to Steiner, whom he met in around 1927. Both were close in age and shared an interest in music; Copland was also deeply fond of Steiner's wife at the time, Mary (who later married architect William Lescaze, another member of this wide circle). Copland included three short art films by Steiner on a Copland-Sessions Concert (1931); Steiner, who had next to no experience making films at this point, "induced" Copland to help him edit one of them. "He claimed he knew nothing about film," recalled Steiner,

> but I persuaded him that a composer should know about unity and progression, and that these had to be important to film editing. Not long ago I saw that film for the first time in almost forty years, and I thought that Aaron and I did not do too well in organization. I

saw that Aaron, in choosing a career of composing rather than film editing, showed splendid judgment.[6]

Propagandizing a progressive, humanistic, and essentially socialist approach to urban planning, *The City* portrays, in visually striking and unusually realistic cinematic terms, four different types of American societies: an old New England village; an industrial factory town and its slums; a metropolitan center; and a "new city" of the sort planned and built by the Resettlement Administration in the late 1930s (the so-called "Greenbelt" towns). Although the film's strong utopian strain fit the tenor of the 1939 World's Fair and its theme, "The World of Tomorrow," some sensitive viewers who loved the film, including the music, had ambiguous feelings about the "new city." Edward Weston, for example, wrote to Van Dyke: "perhaps the artist can only want Utopia for others." Van Dyke explained to Weston that he and Steiner wanted a shorter ending, but that the city planners they had collaborated with "said that that part was what they had made the picture for, that we had had our fun with the first part, and they were going to do the ending as they wanted it."[7] In any case, the filmmakers had noble motives and the principles espoused by the film – decent housing, good medical care, and a healthy environment for all citizens – remained central tenets of the political left.

Copland, who spoke well of the film's "human intimacy,"[8] composed music for nearly all of its forty-five minutes, thus producing a score of about the same length as most of his later feature films. The music effectively matches the film's changing moods and locales: pastoral and quietly dignified for the New England village; brittle and desolate for the industrial wasteland and its slums; hectic and restive for the bustling downtown; jaunty for the Sunday getaway; and joyful and idyllic for the "new city." The

Sunday outing music is a close if more ironic cousin to the final march of *From Sorcery to Science*, while the "new city" music derives from the tender "Dove Dance" from Copland's ballet, *Hear Ye! Hear Ye!*. More distinctive and memorable is the haunting melody that accompanies the poor children of the mill town and the inner city. Copland obviously regarded his music for the New England village and the Sunday outing as of special intrinsic interest, for he excerpted these as "New England Countryside" and "Sunday Traffic" for his suite, *Music for Movies* (1942). However, the score in its entirety contained many ingenious subtleties and picturesque touches, and rightly won wide critical acclaim, including a review in *The New Yorker*, which praised not only its "bitter," "clangy," and "jocular" moments, but its "pensive quality" and "optimism" as well.[9] The music also earned the deep thanks of Van Dyke himself.[10]

The City opened up the door to Hollywood for Copland. After viewing the film at the home of a friend, producer-director Lewis Milestone — the cousin of violinist Nathan Milstein and an accomplished director who was considerably more savvy about music than most movie people — immediately resolved to hire Copland for his film adaptation of John Steinbeck's *Of Mice and Men* (1939), co-produced with Hal Roach. This picture would prove a triumph for all involved, earning Copland his first Academy Award nomination.

Written off by Hollywood as a non-entity only a few years before, Copland now found himself in some demand. However, he had no intention of becoming a Hollywood composer; he wanted to pursue other kinds of projects as well as to maintain his home in Manhattan. And so he became an independent film composer, picking and choosing his pictures carefully: *Our Town* (1940), *The North Star* (1943), *The Red Pony* (1948), and *The Heiress* (1949). These films provided him with the means to undertake less lucrative projects, such as the Piano Sonata (1941), *Appalachian Spring* (1944), and the Third Symphony (1946), and, in addition, helped pave the way for Hollywood's adoption of more modernist and individual styles than had been its custom. Copland's music for the Fair proved, consequently, not only a turning point in his own career, but a milestone in the history of the American cinema.

NOTES:

1. Aaron Copland to Carlos Chávez, 2 June 1937, Copland Collection at the Library of Congress.

2. William R. Trotter, *Priest of Music: The Life of Dimitri Mitropoulos* (Portland, OR, 1995), p. 145.

3. Susan Key, *"Sweet Melody Over Silent Wave": Depression-Era Radio and the American Composer* (Ph.D. diss., University of Maryland at College Park, 1995), pp. 59-60, 140-141.

4. Aaron Copland and Vivian Perlis, *Copland: 1900 through 1942* (Boston, 1984), p. 288.

5. Although Copland referred to the work as *From Sorcery to Science*, the New York Public Library currently has a sketch score catalogued under Copland's working title, "Music for a Puppet Show." According to this copy, Copland composed the reduced score in a mere five days, May 4-8, 1939.

6. Ralph Steiner, *A Point of View* (Middletown, CT, 1978), pp. 12, 14.

7. Leslie Squyres Calmes, *The Letters Between Edward Weston and Willard Van Dyke* (Tucson, 1992), pp. 37-40.

8. Copland and Perlis, *Copland*, p. 290.

9. Robert A. Simon, "Mr. Copland Here, There, and at the Fair," *The New Yorker* 15/16 (3 June 1939): 58.

10. Calmes, *The Letters*, p. 40.

FROM **SORCERY** TO **SCIENCE:**

REMO BUFANO

and

WORLD'S FAIR PUPPET THEATER

John BELL

THE 1939 NEW YORK WORLD'S FAIR HAS LONG BEEN SEEN AS A PIVOTAL MOMENT IN TWENTI-ETH-CENTURY AMERICAN CULTURE. It was not only a "transition point, a prism between the pre- and post-war worlds," but a moment when the dominant elements of twentieth-century American culture – cars, television, advertising – first appeared on a massive, public scale as a premonition of the future.[1] The theme of the Fair was "The World of Tomorrow," and the businessmen and government officials who produced it felt the event should

> demonstrate that betterment of our future American life which may be achieved through the coordinated efforts of Industry, Science, and Art. Above all else, it must stress the vastly increased opportunity and the developed mechanical means which the twentieth century has brought to the masses for better living and accompanying human happiness.[2]

Most importantly, the 1939 World's Fair was a performance event at which hundreds of large and small spectacles used and celebrated technology and mass-produced consumer products. It was a massive spectacle involving the talents of such artists as Alexander Calder, Willem de Kooning, Salvador Dali, Billy Rose, Bill "Bojangles" Robinson, Kurt Weill and Aaron Copland, and above all, the performance of objects – dioramas, machines, automobiles, robots, trains, and puppets.[3]

Performance with objects is the theatrical form historically dominated by the art of puppet theater, and there were scores of puppet shows at the fair, including traditional Punch and Judy shows, fairy tales, and puppet operas. But a particular innovation of this fair was the vast number of corporate-sponsored productions, including the Tatterman Company's shows for Dupont and General Electric; the Modern Art Studios' "Libby Marionettes"; a show for Standard Brands by Sue Hasting's Marionettes; and Walter Dorwin Teague's automatons for the Ford Motor Company.[4] It was perhaps inevitable that Remo Bufano, one of the period's foremost puppeteers, would also be involved, in a collaboration with Aaron Copland at the Hall of Pharmacy entitled *From Sorcery to Science*.

AN AVANT-GARDE PUPPETEER

In 1939, Remo Bufano was forty-five years old, and one of the most celebrated puppeteers in the United States. Born in Italy, Bufano had grown up in New York's Greenwich Village with fourteen brothers and sisters. The traditional Sicilian marionette theaters then active in New York's Italian neighborhoods had a strong early influence on him. Performances of the *Orlando Furioso* epic — full of knights, beautiful warrior maidens, battles, romance, sorcerers, and outspoken didactic portrayals of great moral and religious conflicts — inspired the young Bufano to create his own version of the puppet show at home, and provided an introduction to the art that would become the focus of his life.

In his twenties, Bufano became intimately involved with the "Little Theater" movement that gave rise to American avant-garde performance. In Greenwich Village he acted and worked backstage with the Washington Square Players, the Provincetown Players, and the politically radical New Playwrights Theater.

Bufano also continued making and performing puppet shows of his own: he and his wife Florence performed *Orlando Furioso* and works from the early modern repertoire of puppet theater, such as Arthur Schnitzler's *Gallant Cassian*, for both humble and sophisticated audiences.

In Europe experiments with puppets and masks had been vital cultural events since the 1890s, evidenced in works by Alfred Jarry, Maurice Maeterlinck, Pablo Picasso, Jean Cocteau, the Ballets Russes and the Ballets Suédois. The possibility that puppet performance could become a legitimate modern theater also inspired New York artists. Bufano became part of New York's active puppet theater community of the twenties and thirties, a group that included Tony Sarg, Lou Bunin, and Zuni Maud and Yosl Cutler's Yiddish Modicut Theater, and that shared a conscious need to create a twentieth-century puppet theater as a serious art form for all audiences. Bufano created incidental puppets for numerous Broadway shows, including puppets and masks for Eva Le Gallienne's 1932 production of *Alice in Wonderland*, and a show-stopping 35-foot-tall marionette for Billy Rose's 1935 circus musical *Jumbo*. A Guggenheim fellowship allowed him to study puppet theater in Europe, after which he wrote a number of "how-to" puppet books for children. Through the League of Composers, he designed and built puppets for two operas: Manuel de Falla's *El Retablo de Maese Pedro* (1924), and Igor Stravinsky's *Oedipus Rex* (1931). As a result of this ground-breaking work, Bufano became New York's most celebrated avant-garde puppeteer, famous for his rough-hewn but inspired productions. In a 1926 essay for *The Little Review* he optimistically proclaimed that America would become the center of a modern "renaissance of the marionette."[5]

During the Depression, Bufano was called to head the popular New York marionette unit of the Federal

Theater Project, but quit in 1937, protesting "obstructive policies" which hindered his work.[6] By 1939, Bufano had even begun to experiment in the new medium that would change the nature of American puppet theater most profoundly: televison.

THE HALL OF PHARMACY

The 1939 World's Fair featured pavilions representing major United States corporations and countries around the world. The Hall of Pharmacy was built so that a consortium of twenty-one American pharmaceutical companies including Ex-Lax, Gillette, the Bristol-Myers Company, the Kalak Water Company, and the Schering Corporation could, as the *New York Times* put it, trace "mankind's efforts for comfort and health down the ages."[7] The consortium called on Bufano to create a show "dramatizing man's pursuit of health." In response to their commission, Bufano created an epic commercial spectacle using only giant puppets – something never before seen on a New York stage.[8]

The Hall of Pharmacy was located only a few hundred yards away from the Trylon and Perisphere, which marked the center of the Fair. Situated on the corner of the "Street of Wings" and the "Court of Power," the Hall of Pharmacy was significantly much closer to the Hall of Industry, the Electric Utilities Pavilion, and other buildings in the Production and Distribution Zone than it was to the Medicine and Public Health Pavilion; its location clearly conveyed its ultimate purpose – to connect consumers with products. The building was divided into three sections: a "Drugstore of Yesterday," a combination "Drugstore of Tomorrow" and "Soda Fountain of the Future," and the "World's Largest Medicine Chest." The Medicine Chest section consisted of an auditorium about forty-five feet wide and at least 100 feet long, with a twenty-foot-tall ceiling and, at one end, a theater stage. Exhibitions in this room presented the history of medicine and drugs as a slow march of progress leading to the wonders of modern pharmacy created by American companies. According to a *New York Times* reporter, "a tabloid history of the science of pharmacy" was displayed in a series of friezes mounted on the walls of the room, ranging "from 'Anepu,' the mythological fox-headed apothecary, to the gods of Egypt, down to the modern laboratory where sulphapyridine and other microbe killers are brewed in test tubes." This history was complemented by "individual booths along the sides of the theater," where "various manufacturers of drugs and cosmetics" had their own displays.[9]

The focal point of the Hall of Pharmacy was its Medicine Chest theater, combining a rather traditional proscenium opening with a thirty-foot-diameter turntable stage large enough to house Bufano's twelve-foot-tall figures, advertised (with conventional fairground hyperbole) as "the largest puppets in the world."[10] Donald Deskey designed the theater to look like "the largest bathroom-type medicine cabinet in the world" by giving its proscenium arch the graceful curve of a medicine cabinet door, an effect intensified by a large pane of reflecting glass covering the stage opening.[11] During performances sidelighting made the glass transparent, but between shows the glass became a mirror reflecting Gillette, Bromo-Seltzer, Listerine, Phillips, Saraka, and Ipana displays for the potential consumers gathered there.

It is important to note the ways in which the Hall of Pharmacy stage was similar to the Sicilian marionette theaters Bufano had grown up seeing on the Lower East Side. Deskey and Bufano's innovation was simple but theatrically brilliant: instead of working with puppets half the size of humans, they created the stage and puppets on a stupendous scale, in keeping with the grandiose physical and rhetorical dimensions of the Fair. An even stronger connection to the *Orlando Furioso* traditions was forged in the straightforward manner in which *From Sorcery to Science* told its story; its didactic style was close to the rhetoric of moral certainty characteristic of the medieval mystery plays, fairground shows, and puppet theaters that transmitted the central tenets of Christian European convictions. In the 1930s this style was most vividly represented in agit-prop theater and advertising copy, and it was the dominant language of the World's Fair.

Like many other performances at the Fair, *From Sorcery to Science* ran on an assembly-line schedule, to present continual performances for a constantly changing audience primed to see one attraction after another. Five puppeteers worked in rotating pairs, operating Bufano's giant figures from the "dizzy height" of a bridge at least fifteen feet above the stage floor.[12] The aural element of the production also reflected the new machine-like aesthetics: Aaron Copland's orchestral music and the narration, recited by radio celebrity Lowell Thomas, were heard by way of the novel means of a pre-recorded soundtrack.

From Sorcery to Science lasted only about ten minutes, but it functioned as a live recapitulation of the progress-through-technology theme fairgoers saw endlessly reiterated throughout the fairgrounds. The *New York Times* called it a "contribution to the scientific education of the Fair-goer," and above all else the show taught modern pharmacy by defining what it was not: a succession of ineffective, unenlightened folk medicines created by a variety of "primitives," including a Chinese doctor, a female witch, a medieval alchemist, and an African Witch Doctor. The counterpoint to these characters was "two modern scientists [and] a modern druggist," who would trump earlier benighted efforts not only by inventing new drugs and cosmetics, but by delivering them to the central figure of the show, a consumer in the form of "a modern beautiful girl."[13]

The first scene presented Bufano's version of "an old Chinese doctor's medicine shop" from the Ming Dynasty.[14] While Copland's music featured pentatonic "Chinese" melodies, and Bufano's Chinese doctor puppet labored over a potion, Thomas's narrative described the shop as a place full of "bats, dragons, bones, magic spells and mystery," whose proprietor could provide only partial comfort to his patients. "He knew something of herbs, he could help some of those who came to him," Thomas announced, "but the days of modern science and research were still way off."

In Scene Two, *From Sorcery to Science* shifted to Europe, and the cavern of a Witch who chanted spells lifted from Shakespeare's *Macbeth*. Bufano's puppet for this scene was the largest in the show — a huge, ugly seven-foot-tall woman's head with cloth sleeves connected to two large hands. Her manner was monstrous: *Life* magazine wrote that "her tongue retracts, her nose waggles and her mouth drools globules of liquid rubber."[15] According to Aaron Copland, she also had "an eye that lit up and popped."[16] The Witch's nostrums were, again, presented as exotic mixtures of doubtful practical purpose. "Brewing her secret potions in dark caverns, shrouding her every deed in mystery," Thomas intoned, "the witch cast her spells." But, like the Chinese doctor, this folk healer had only partial success. "How pitiful it was," Thomas would say, "when she failed."

Scene Three featured a twelve-foot-tall Alchemist with a "hawk-faced" papier-mâché head, two bony papier-mâché hands, and a velvet robe with a long chain for a belt.[17] While Copland's music provided modal harmonies and mysterious dissonances, the narration defined this European mystic's work as a small step forward for medicine. The Alchemist "was wiser than the others," Thomas

explained, "he experimented and knew something of the chemistry of his day." However, despite his knowledge and his "smoky retreats and fiery crucibles," the Alchemist failed to make gold. "Progress," Thomas concluded, "comes slowly."

In the fourth scene, the play turned to an exotic, "primitive" Africa cultivated by pre-war American popular culture, only a few decades removed from the racist minstrel show traditions of the previous century. This Africa was the milieu of Orson Welles's 1936 "voodoo" *Macbeth*; of the *Swing Mikado* starring Bill "Bojangles" Robinson (a huge hit also playing at the Fair); and of Eugene O'Neill's *The Emperor Jones*, the 1920 production by Bufano's old colleagues at the Provincetown Playhouse. Bufano's pop-culture Africa was, paradoxically, mysterious and dangerous as well as humorous and tame. His African Witch Doctor was the most striking design of the show, with a largely naked, brightly painted, and fully articulated body, including large feet and hands and many copper and wooden bracelets. Its puppet head wore a large, two-horned "African" demon mask. While Bufano's Witch Doctor danced to Copland's conga-tinged syncopations, Lowell Thomas exclaimed:

> Why even today, savages of darkest Africa go to the witch doctor....These unfortunate people never heard of anything else but the beating of drums, of superstition and magic. Voodoo! These savages are to be pitied...because they live now, when other people enjoy the benefits of health and happiness.

By Scene Five of *From Sorcery to Science,* Hall of Pharmacy audiences must have been primed for the inevitable conclusion to the short drama: the American drugstore as the rational, progressive alternative to primitive and alien practices. The culminating scene was performed in two parts. First, Bufano presented a "modern laboratory" staffed by "modern scientists": two clean-cut, fair-complexioned men in white medical uniforms concocting modern medicines (or perhaps health and beauty aids).[18] The scene, Lowell Thomas's recorded voice specified, represented not simply these particular characters, but a whole class of pioneers, "thousands of men and women: chemists, doctors, dentists and biologists" of "America today," who, definitely "not with Voodoo," were making it possible for American citizens to enjoy "health, beauty and cleanliness." The second part of Scene Five took place in a drug store, "where a druggist tells a housewife what protection from disease and infection her modern drug store gives her."[19] The play ended at the point of purchase: the "modern druggist" selling the "modern beautiful girl" the products that would enable her to maintain her modern American way of life.[20]

But the end of the show was not the end of the performance at the Hall of Pharmacy. When Copland's music and the giant puppets faded away, the glass once more became a mirror in which the audience could see not only themselves but the continuing spectacle of pharmaceutical products all around them, a spectacle that continued as the audience made their way to the Drugstore of the Future next door and then to the other commercial pavilions, which all reinforced the fairgoers' identity as modern American consumers.

PUPPETS AND
THE PERFORMANCE OF AMERICAN CULTURE

The 1939 World's Fair was a pivotal moment in the performance of American culture. While in Europe the experiments in puppet modernism were centered on moral, social, and political issues, what characterized similar experiments in the United States turned out to be the overwhelming power of commercial culture – the relation of art to commerce. In this sense, performance at the World's Fair was the precursor to American business theater of the rest of the century: the "industrials," commercial exhibitions, theme parks, and, above all, the advertising that now saturates cultural space.

The gigantic scale of commercial performance at the World's Fair was new and exciting, but also, to many people, alarming. The New Jersey Pharmaceutical Association, for example, issued a resolution condemning the Hall of Pharmacy's use of traditional pharmacy symbols to sell products. Manifesting a healthy outrage that seems almost quaint today, an Association spokesman said, "we thought it was going to be a scientific exhibition, but instead we find it commercialized by hideous signs advertising proprietary products."[21]

Frank Worth, a visiting English puppeteer who saw *From Sorcery to Science*, found Copland's music "stirring" and Bufano's puppets "truly American in size." But after seeing other similarly sponsored puppet shows, Worth "came away from the fair with a feeling that, although equipment was excellent and spending lavish, the sponsored puppets were merely animated shop-window dummies, which may have sold things, but certainly were not the best in puppetry."[22] This was a sentiment echoed by Paul McPharlin, the most respected American puppeteer of the time, who wrote in his journal *Puppetry* that the World's Fair puppet shows

> set a new high for artistic and technical excellence too. But what did they have to say as puppets? 'Buy Jell-o' and 'Use Lucite'! And they were not, in all the shows, even entertaining saying it. This cannot be blamed on the puppeteers so much as the advertisers they worked for. But this is clear:

the general public has never supported puppets so handsomely as the advertisers did at this fair, and the puppeteers are quick to know which side their bread is buttered on.

The fact that McPharlin, Worth, and the New Jersey pharmacists expressed such affront at the mix of art and commerce at the 1939 World's Fair indicates how startling that cultural combination was. Remo Bufano, like other American artists of the time, was challenged to forge the modern shape of his medium from old techniques and new technologies. This process was inextricably tied to the powerful and troubling dynamics of the art/commerce relationship, which will inevitably continue to define the development of puppetry and other American arts.

NOTES

Research assistance for this article was provided by Laura Helton

1. Joseph Philip Cusker, *The World of Tomorrow: The 1939 World's Fair*, (Ph.D. diss., Rutgers University, 1990), p. 2.

2. Robert D. Kohn, "A Fair for the Man in the Street," Memorandum submitted to the World's Fair Board of Design, as quoted by Cusker, *The World of Tomorrow*, p. 26.

3. For a fascinating contemporary account of World's Fair performance, see Morton Eustis, "Big Show in Flushing Meadows," *Theatre Arts Monthly* 23/7 (July 1939): 566-577. See also Richard Wurts, *The New York World's Fair in 155 Photographs* (New York, 1977).

4. In contrast to these corporate shows, *The Story of Ferdinand* and *String Fever*, performed in the WPA Building at the World's Fair by the marionette division of the Federal Theater Project, were cancelled in June 1939 after Congress liquidated the F.T.P. for what it called "subversive influences" within the arts project. See *Dawn of a New Day. The New York World's Fair*, exh. cat., Queens Museum (Flushing, NY, 1980), p. 87.

5. Remo Bufano, "The Marionette in the Theater," *The Little Review* 11/2 (Winter 1926): 42.

6. "Bufano Quits WPA Unit," *New York Times* (15 Nov. 1937): 8.

7. "Hall of Pharmacy Opens," *New York Times* (13 May 1939): 8.

8. "These Are Giant Puppets," *Life* (1 May 1939): 7.

9. "Pharmacist's Art of Ages Depicted," *New York Times* (30 May 1939): 12.

10. "Pharmacy Hall Depicts Fight for Comfort and Health," *Today at the Fair* (16 May 1939).

11. "World's Fair Gets Medicine Cabinet Stage," Unidentified newspaper article, Remo Bufano clipping file, New York Public Library, Dance Collection.

12. Frank Worth, "Impressions of American Puppetry," *Puppetry* 10 (1939): 5.

13. "Pharmacist's Art," 12.

14. This and subsequent quotations from the narration of *From Sorcery to Science* are taken from a 1997 transcription made by Jonathan Sheffer, from a tape of the original performance in the Library of Congress.

15. "Giant Puppets," 7.

16. "Giant Puppets," 7; and Aaron Copland and Vivian Perlis, *Copland: 1900 through 1942* (Boston, 1984), p. 288.

17. Copland and Perlis, *Copland*, p. 288.

18. Copland and Perlis, *Copland*, p. 288; "Pharmacist's Art," 12.

19. "Pharmacist's Art," 12.

20. Copland and Perlis, *Copland*, p. 288.

21. "Criticize Pharmacy Hall: Jersey Pharmacists Decry Use of 'Commercial' Signs," *New York Times* (1 July 1939): 20.

22. Worth, "Impressions," 5.

23. Paul McPharlin, "The Puppet Decade in America," *Puppetry* 10 (1939): 3.

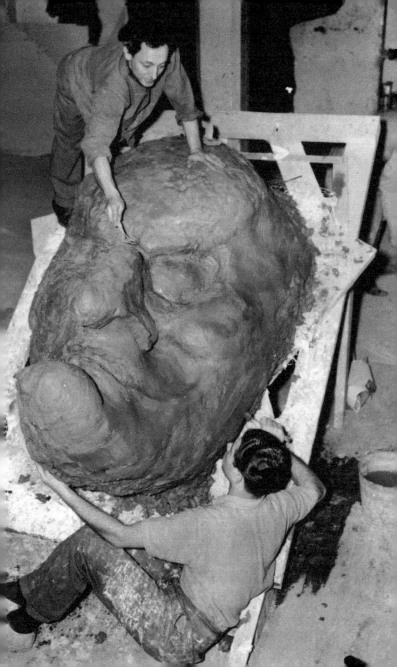

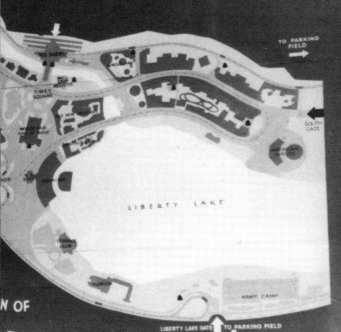

STATE EXHIBITS
GENERAL EXHIBITS
TRANSPORTATION EXHIBITS
AMUSEMENTS
RESTAURANTS
RESTAURANTS WITHIN EXHIBIT BUILDINGS
GENERAL UTILITIES & PRIVATE BUILDINGS
BUS ROUTES
BUS STATIONS
LOUNGE CAR ROUTES-STOP ON SIGNAL
REST ROOMS

TO PARKING FIELD

SOUTH GATE

AMERICAN JUBILEE

TIMES SQUARE

LIBERTY LAKE

TERRACE CLUB

FLORIDA

ARMY CAMP

LIBERTY LAKE GATE   TO PARKING FIELD

N OF

RLD'S FAIR OF 1940

PLATE I

PLATE
II

MAN = *chemicals* = **FOOD**

PLATE III

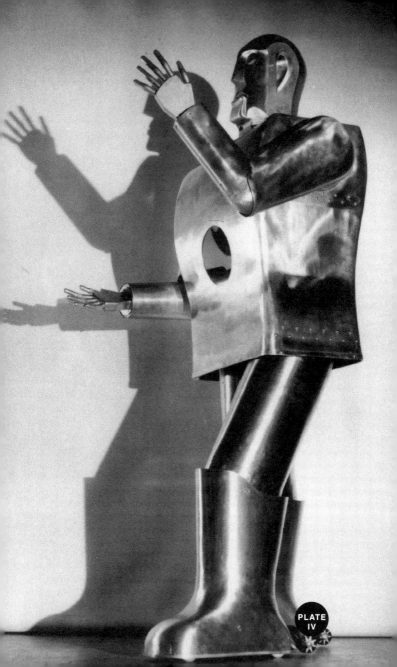

PLATE
IV

PLATE
V

PLATE
VI

NEW YORK WORLD'S FAIR 1939

· DANIEL C.C. GILBERT ·

PLATE
VII

PLATE
IX

PLATE
X

PLATE
XI

PLATE
XII

ARCHITECTURAL MODERNISMS AT THE FAIR

Rosemarie **HAAG BLETTER**

THE ARCHITECTURE AND ENTERTAINMENT OF THE NEW YORK WORLD'S FAIR OF 1939 HAS ATTAINED NEAR CULT STATUS, BOTH IN ITS OWN DAY AND AS A VIVIDLY REMEMBERED EVENT. It continues to exercise a hold on the imagination of those that saw it in a way that has not been rivaled by later World's Fairs. The great streamlined pavilions with their futuristic rides provided not only a respite from the Depression but an impressive model for a better tomorrow as well. The art historian Robert Rosenblum, who encountered the fair at the age of twelve, recalls it as seeming "like something out of Buck Rogers or Flash Gordon."[1]

In fact, the theme of the fair was "Building the World of Tomorrow"[2] and the success of the fair depended on its carefully constructed image of progress. Progress was a concept that had been held up as a solution for an improved future throughout the worst years of the Depression, but it had never before been realized in such palpable form, and as such eye-catching, startling buildings.

By far the most popular exhibit at the fair was in the large General Motors Pavilion designed by Albert Kahn, a noted architect of state-of-the-art industrial plants for several Detroit car manufacturers. In the late twenties and early thirties the Soviet Union had even engaged his firm for assistance in the construction of new factories.[3]

The General Motors Pavilion was actually a group of four buildings, gathered behind a huge, dramatic, diagonal wall that curved back on itself. A vertical slash down the middle of this wall provided the mysterious entry point for long lines of visitors, who traveled via a curving ramp into the interior exhibits, called "Highways and Horizons." The focus of these displays was the "Futurama" by industrial designer Norman Bel Geddes, who was Kahn's collaborator in the General Motors Pavilion. The Futurama fulfilled most completely the utopian, visionary underpinnings common among international exhibitions. It contained a large model of a metropolis with streamlined skyscrapers interspersed between low-rise buildings, parks, and criss-crossing superhighways that spread out into the American countryside, and projected a future in which seven-lane highways, designed to accommodate traffic moving at 100 miles per hour, were commonplace. In terms of planning, it combined the urbanistic projects of the twenties by Le Corbusier with Frank Lloyd Wright's scheme for Broadacre City, begun in the mid-thirties. Broadacre was more rural than Le Corbusier's plans, yet both architects had relied heavily on the highway as the connective tissue of their communities. In the Futurama, visitors circled the 35,000 square-foot panoramic model in chairs that functioned as a kind of skyride. A taped message from the sound-equipped chairs informed the audience that such a design would benefit industrial communities as well as farmers and that "the city of 1960, with its abundant sunshine, fresh air, fine green parkways [is] all the result of thoughtful planning and design."[4] The Futurama predicted that some 38 million cars would be in use by the year 1960; in fact, the count at that time turned out to be double the projected figure. In the actual future, car manufacturers were even more successful in selling cars to the public than they themselves had expected.

The urbanism proposed in the Futurama was not so different from that on display in the Theme Center — the Trylon and Perisphere, designed by Harrison & Fouilhoux. The diorama of Democracity by the industrial designer Henry Dreyfuss, inside the Perisphere, similarly combined the metropolis with its superhighways and sub-urbanized settings (this exhibit was accompanied by a musical score by William Grant Still conducted by Andre Kostelanetz).[5] The real difference between the two models was that the Futurama's plan was unabashedly focused on a future filled with cars and highways. This was borne out even more explicitly in a full-scale mock-up of an urban intersection created by the four structures making up the General Motors group of buildings. The "street level" of this intersection was filled with new General Motors cars and elevated walkways. Bridges above this crossing were for pedestrian traffic, and separated cars and pedestrians in a way that had been proposed in ideal designs by planners for decades. The pleasant distraction of the Futurama was followed by the impact of the core of the General Motors display, where streets were filled with cars.

By comparison with the General Motors Pavilion's sweeping, abstracted exterior forms, the profile of the Ford Motor Company's Pavilion seemed less futuristic and more of its own time: the Moderne-style entrance included glass bricks in its curving window strip, and the whole was capped by a large stainless steel figure of Mercury by Robert Foster. The Ford Pavilion, like its General Motors counterpart, was designed by Albert Kahn, but here he worked with the industrial designer Walter Dorwin Teague. The most notable feature of this pavilion was a half-mile highway with moving cars. The road exited from the pavilion proper, curved around a "garden court" and spiraled upward in great decreasing loops — a spiral that defined one end of the Ford display — and then proceeded at an upper level back to the building. Visitors could test actual Fords, Mercurys, and Lincoln-Zephyrs on this dynamically conceived "Road of Tomorrow." The Garden Court, encircled by this road, was the setting for composer Ferde Grofé and his musicians' performance on Novachords.[6] In both the General Motors and the Ford Pavilions, the telling features were not the streamlined buildings themselves, but the futuristic highways that defined the architecture. In this respect these buildings in the fair's Transportation Zone predicted the future more accurately than did their individual forms.

Most of the commercial pavilions at the World's Fair invoked aspects of the older Art Deco style of the twenties or the Streamlined Moderne style of the thirties. In many instances, these two popular "Modernisms" were conflated. This was true of the Schaefer Center by Eggers and Higgins, a large restaurant seating 1600 patrons, or the National Dairy Products Corporation Building by De Witt Clinton Pond, both in the fair's Food Zone. Art Deco and Moderne were not avant-garde styles; they were popular modernisms. They borrowed motifs from several high styles of early twentieth-century Modernism, such as Futurism, Expressionism, and Cubism, which were commonly grafted onto a more traditional massing as decorative elements.[7] As in Manhattan's Chrysler and/or Empire State Buildings, modernity served as a public relations tool, mediated by sensuous, theatrical forms that kept it from being off-putting and difficult. At the same time, Art Deco and Streamlined Moderne clearly were more "jazzy" than the traditional Beaux-Arts styles. They were thus particularly appropriate as a commercial idiom, positioned midway between the avant-garde and true conservatism.

It is important to acknowledge that the New York World's Fair was dominated by its commercial pavilions because it was not an official world's fair. The fair com-

mittee had wanted to extend the exhibitions over the span of two years, from 1939 to 1940, in order to break even financially. However, the international organization that oversees these events did not give its approval because world's fairs are limited to one-year events. In part for this reason, but primarily because of the economic exigencies and growing political tensions in Europe, the late thirties were not auspicious years for engaging in such an expansive exercise in public relations for many foreign countries. A few countries participated in the fair, but not as many as one might have expected at an official world's fair.

Two of the foreign pavilions were among the most avant-garde designs. The Brazilian Pavilion by Lucio Costa and Oscar Niemeyer—in the fifties both were associated with the design of Brasilia—with its ramp and perforated sunscreen, was influenced by Le Corbusier, who had visited Brazil in the thirties. But a large biomorphic cut-out in its roof also gave this pavilion a more playful feeling, which reflected the initial interplay between Surrealism and the more ascetic Modernism of the twenties. A softening of classic Modernism's orthogonal forms was also present in the Finnish Pavilion by Alvar Aalto. The warm, textured design of this pavilion's exterior, with its vertical wooden slats, revealed a Scandinavian version of Modernism that had never closely adhered to the white-washed surfaces that are conventionally associated with the International Style of the twenties. The great display wall of the interior, also done in the same textured material, was designed as an animated, undulating surface. Here the architectural expression was completely removed from the technocentric symbolism of both a high-style Modernism and the more populist Streamlined Moderne. Instead, it embraced an imagery associated with emotive and primarily anthropocentric qualities. Aalto's influence in particular, as well as a general adoption of Scandinavian Modern, gained significance after World War II, in the context of a broader redefinition of the cerebral International Style.

On the other hand, a thoroughly conservative architectural style was evident in some of the international pavilions, as well as in most of the buildings erected by federal and state agencies. Both the U.S.S.R. Pavilion by Boris Iofan and Karo S. Alabian and the Italian Pavilion by Michele Busiri-Vici were highly melodramatic examples of an abstracted classicism. The United States (Federal) Building by Howard L. Cheney more closely resembled the pared-down classicism common in federal buildings in Washington, D.C. of the thirties and forties. The architecture of the Court of States, in which 23 states and Puerto Rico were represented, was more broadly historicizing. Several of the structures look loosely Georgian in their combination of exterior brick- and stone -work. Some of the state pavilions were replicas of regional historic monuments. In fact, aside from the Amusement Zone, this was the only context in which the fair's Design Board allowed the presence of replicas,[8] because the fair was intended to highlight only the new and the future.

One other area of the New York World's Fair that did not embrace the streamlined sleekness of the commercial pavilions was the "Town of Tomorrow," an area that showcased residential buildings. Of the fifteen houses in the fair's Tomorrow Town, as it was also called, only four had flat roofs and even came close to a kind of modernism; the others veered between Colonial, Regency, and other historicizing styles. Tomorrow Town was intended as a full-scale model village. While it had the look of suburbia, paradoxically it was advertised in the fair's literature as a recreation of a New England village: "Tomorrow Town...A new concept in community planning that will aid in re-creating the old New England type of village universally acknowledged as the most perfect form of democracy..."

Although Tomorrow Town was primarily retrospective in style, modernity took over in the state-of-the-art mechanical equipment and kitchens. Typical of this disjunction between exterior conservatism and internal mechanical futurism is the Kelvin Home:

> With its quaint charm and quiet hospitality, the Kelvin Home breathes the spirit of New England's hallowed days. Yet step inside – and the world of tomorrow awaits you. Daily living brought to the effortless, automatic perfection made possible by the complete electrical home equipment of the Nash-Kelvinator Corporation.

In contrast, across from Tomorrow Town the streamlined future was expressed more coherently in the Crane Exhibit, where the latest developments in heating and plumbing were on display. While the commercial pavilions exhibited modernity like peacocks, residential design, even in the futuristic setting of the fair, remained quite traditional.[9] Such differing approaches to commercial and residential buildings had been common outside the fair as well. When Albert Kahn, architect of the General Motors and Ford Pavilions, and of many advanced manufacturing plants for the car industry, was asked to build private houses for the same clients, he designed extremely traditional stone mansions. Attitudes surrounding the idea of the home tended to be controlled by psychological ties to tradition, security, and protection, while modernity and an image of futurism were at the same time found appropriate for commercial buildings.

There was, to be sure, a great deal of spirited entertainment in the official sections of the fair, such as the Transportation Zone with the General Motors Futurama, or the pageant, "Railroads on Parade" in the Railroads exhibit, with a musical score by Kurt Weill. For most fairgoers, however, the bawdier and more informal shows of the Entertainment Zone – with its bathing-suit beauty contests, or topless mermaids swimming in a tank of water, recalled in E.L. Doctorow's *World's Fair* of 1985 – were among the highlights. Salvador Dali's "Dream of Venus" pavilion, with its soft, undulating forms and figures of bare-breasted mermaids apparently caught in openings of its cave-like walls, conjoined the uninhibited display of the erotic with an appropriate architectural form.

The Entertainment Zone, however, was more like a fun-fair and about the here and now, and had little to do with the fair's futuristic motto, "Building the World of Tomorrow." Futuristic prediction was the bailiwik of commercial corporations such as the Radio Corporation of America, whose pavilion, designed by Skidmore and Owings (who, as Skidmore, Owings & Merrill, would become one of the largest post-war Modernist firms) was shaped like a radio tube. Inside, new RCA television sets were displayed. Public commercial broadcasting had begun with the opening of the fair and took place for about two hours a week.[10] Although the General Motors Futurama received more attention at the time of the fair, cars represented an already established technology, while the television sets lined up inside the RCA Pavilion represented the overwhelming change that would occur after the war in the way visual information in particular and information technology in general would affect every home.

NOTES

1. Robert Rosenblum, "Remembrance of Fairs Past," *Remembering the Future. The New York World's Fair from 1939 to 1964* (New York, 1989), p. 12.

2. Stanley Appelbaum, *The New York World's Fair 1939/1940* (New York, 1977), p. 3. See also, for its insightful essays, Helen Harrison et al., *Dawn of a New Day. The New York World's Fair, 1939/40* (New York, 1980) and, for further illustrations, Larry Zim et al., *The World of Tomorrow. The 1939 New York World's Fair* (New York, 1988).

3. Federico Bucci, *Albert Kahn. Architect of Ford* (New York, 1991).

4. Rosemarie Haag Bletter, "The 'Laissez-Faire,' Good Taste, and Money Trees. Architecture at the Fair," in *Remembering the Future*, p. 114.

5. Appelbaum, *New York World's Fair*, p. 3.

6. Appelbaum, *New York World's Fair*, p. 23.

7. Cervin Robinson and Rosemarie Haag Bletter, *Skyscraper Style. Art Deco New York* (New York, 1975).

8. Appelbaum, *New York World's Fair*, p. 106.

9. Rosemarie Haag Bletter, "The World of Tomorrow. The Future with a Past," in *High Styles. Twentieth-Century American Design* (New York, 1985), pp. 93-94.

10. Appelbaum, *New York World's Fair*, p. 44.

1939: A FAIR **YEAR**

FOR **POPULAR SONGS**

Miles KREUGER

IF THE TASTE OF A SOCIETY DICTATES
THE STYLE OF ITS POPULAR MUSIC, THE
SONGS OF 1939 OFFER A VIVID PICTURE OF WHAT
AMERICANS WERE THINKING AND FEELING
TOWARD THE END OF THAT TURBULENT DECADE.
During the first half of the 1930s, with the
Depression at its deepest, most of the songs Americans
sang came from movies and Broadway shows. But it was
Broadway that set the style.

At a time when an entire family could afford to be
fed, housed, and clothed on twenty-five dollars a week,
even the two- or three-dollar admission to a Broadway
musical was forbiddingly expensive to many. Thus, the theatre became a playground for the well-to-do. In a nation
where everyone listened to the same radio programs and
read the same newspapers and magazines, everyone got
the point of every joke. In effect, every joke was an inside
joke, and the entire American electorate was "inside."

With theatre largely available to those with
money, Broadway in a sense evolved into something of a
social club. The songs in revues and musical comedies
were peppered with topical references to people, events,
and trends; and everyone understood. The imagery in love
songs could be exotic ("Begin the Beguine"), the references
chichi ("You're a Bendel bonnet"), and singers distinctly
upper class ("... in my pet pailletted gown"). The more stun-
ningly garbed the players were, the more attractive they
seemed. The musicals of the early 1930s were distinctly
seen from the perspective of the penthouse, looking down
at the tenements below.

By the middle of the decade, two things occurred to change the point of view of popular songs and concomitantly their very style of presentation. The economy improved, and swing bands took over from solo singers.

On August 21, 1935, at the Palomar Ballroom in Los Angeles, Benny Goodman and His Orchestra were received with such ardent acclaim, that the swing era simply exploded and engulfed popular music. The public, particularly the youngsters, shifted their allegiance from solo vocalists to the bands. Bing Crosby, Alice Faye, Judy Garland, Rudy Vallee, and others were still selling records because they were big movie or radio personalities, but the stars on commercial phonograph records were Goodman, the Dorsey brothers, Glenn Miller, Larry Clinton, Woody Herman, and the other bands with their distinctive, trademark arrangements.

Swing was democratic. Couples could jitterbug on Park Avenue or in the most squalid slums. From coast to coast, swing was the sound of the times.

In the late 1950s, when rock and roll substantially wiped out popular music, Broadway songwriters had to accept the grim reality that, for the first time, their songs were not those being sung by the general public. This phenomenon was so threatening that some of the most prestigious Broadway bards tried in vain to sound "hip," while others, like Harold Arlen, simply stepped aside to allow a younger generation to take over.

Back in 1939, the Broadway composers had to accept that all types of show tunes, from ballads to comic ditties, were fair game for the swing shift. In the hit 1939 musical *Too Many Girls*, Lorenz Hart indulged with two sarcastic digs at the trend. He wrote "swing bands give you heebie-jeebies" and then dedicated the entire song "I Like To Recognize the Tune" to a meticulous demolition of the effect of the bands on melody. Unlike the rock era twenty

years later, at least the bands were recording show tunes, despite their often highly altered form.

Sad to say, the Broadway musical provided very few distinguished or enduring songs during 1939. Throughout the Depression, shows featured at least fifteen substantial hits during any calender year. In 1939, the number was barely half a dozen.

The year on Broadway began January 18 with Noël Coward's revue *Set to Music*, its score largely reprised from London productions and familiar to most theatregoers. There were however two new gems, "I'm So Weary of It All" and "I Went to a Marvellous Party," both essentially special material for that glorious clown, Beatrice Lillie.

One for the Money (February 4) had no hits, while *Stars in Your Eyes* (February 9) had two splendid songs by Dorothy Fields and Arthur Schwartz that deserve to be better remembered: "I'll Pay the Check" and "This Is It." Like all the spring entries, *Stars in Your Eyes* suffered from competition from the World's Fair and closed prematurely, despite the potent presence of Ethel Merman.

Three shows with black casts followed: *Lew Leslie's Blackbirds of 1939* (February 11), the WPA production *The Swing Mikado* (March 1), and Michael Todd's slicker update of the Gilbert and Sullivan masterpiece, *The Hot Mikado* (March 23). After a brief run on Broadway, the last was transferred, with its captivating star Bill Robinson, to the Fair, where it was one of the summer hits.

The long-running *Pins and Needles* was updated with new numbers but no hits (April 20), nor were there any in the Latin revue *Mexicana* (April 21), nor the WPA *Sing for Your Supper* (April 24). The last did however include the cantata "Ballad for Americans" by Earl Robinson and John Latouche. The piece went largely unnoticed until November 5, when Paul Robeson sang it on the CBS network program *Pursuit of Happiness*. The patriotic fervor and fine craftsmanship of the piece made it an instantaneous success, particularly with schools and professional choral groups. Paul Robeson's Victor album was a best-seller for years.

The first real hit song from Broadway did not appear until June 19, when the Brazilian Bombshell, Carmen Miranda, stopped *The Streets of Paris* nightly with her spirited rendition of "South American Way" by Al Dubin and Jimmy McHugh. Her swiveling hips, gleaming smile, and twinkling eyes wafted Miss Miranda to Hollywood and a long-term contract with 20th Century-Fox, where she repeated the song in her first film, *Down Argentine Way*.

A group of Austrian refugees played briefly in *From Vienna* (June 20), followed July 6 by *Yokel Boy*, in which Judy Canova introduced "Comes Love" by Lew Brown, Charles Tobias, and Sammy Stept. The real show-stopper however was the interpolated "Beer Barrel Polka," sung by the Minute Men from Lexington.

The effervescent Scottish lass, Ella Logan, asked the musical question "Are You Havin' Any Fun?" in *George White's Scandals* (August 28), but that perky tune by Jack Yellen and Sammy Fain has been sadly neglected over the years.

Danny Kaye burst onto the Broadway scene in Max Liebman's *The Straw Hat Revue* (September 29). It was in that intimate show that Kaye introduced one of his signature songs, "Anatole of Paris," written by his future wife, Sylvia Fine; but it was not until Kaye performed the ditty in *The Secret Life of Walter Mitty*, the 1947 Goldwyn film, that the general public heard and fell in love with it.

The first long-running musical of the year, *Too Many Girls*, with a score by Rodgers and Hart, did not open until October 18, only thirteen days before the Fair closed for the season. The score contained three substantial hits:

the ballad "I Didn't Know What Time It Was," a continuing favorite today in cabarets, along with "Give It Back to the Indians" and "I Like To Recognize the Tune." All three were widely recorded by the bands, and even Mary Jane Walsh from the original cast made Columbia recordings.

Jerome Kern and Oscar Hammerstein II, two of the theatre's most beloved and highly skilled craftsmen, felt that it was time to offer a valentine to young people trying to break into acting. *Very Warm for May* (November 17) was set in a summer stock playhouse and offered several lovely songs, including the wry "All in Fun." But it was the double duet "All the Things You Are" that garnered the most attention. Many scholars feel that this is the finest popular song of all times; but whether it is or not, "All the Things You Are" remains Broadway's jewel of the year. Unfortunately, the show itself fell victim to endless, mindless rewrites on its pre-Broadway journey to town and folded after a mere fifty-nine performances. It was Kern's final score for the Great White Way.

The two jive Mikados obviously planted a seed, because on November 29, at the huge Center Theatre in Radio City, the international producer Erik Charell presented *Swingin' the Dream*, "a musical variation of Shakespeare's *A Midsummer Night's Dream*," in the words of the Playbill.

With the action shifted to New Orleans at the birth of jazz, the cast overflowed with the hottest names in swing: Benny Goodman and His Sextet, Louis Armstrong, Maxine Sullivan, the Dandridge sisters, Bud Freeman, Max Kaminsky, Peewee Russell, Eddie Condon, Zutty Singleton, and the Deep River Boys. The comics included Jackie "Moms" Mabley, Nicodemus, and Butterfly McQueen.

Goodman recorded "Spring Song," based on Mendelssohn, "Peace, Brother," "Flyin' Home," "Jumpin' at the Woodside," and "Darn That Dream," in addition to other interpolations. Despite all this talent, *Swingin' the Dream* expired after just thirteen performances.

December 6 brought the year's second and final big book show, *Du Barry Was a Lady*, with a score (albeit a second-rate score) by Cole Porter. As Porter became more and more influenced by swing rhythms, a curious change occurred in his writing. His stylish songs of the early thirties had necessitated a literacy and wit with which he was comfortable, and his ballads were skillful explorations of the private depths of the singer's emotions. But swing was sketched with less depth and a more gaudy surface, and this was at odds with everything that Porter stood for as a man and an artist. So with *Du Barry Was a Lady*, the writer revealed the first symptoms of a decline that was to plunge precipitously until his astonishing rebound with *Kiss Me, Kate* in 1948.

Du Barry offered an agreeable but undistinguished love song, "Do I Love You, Do I?," the funny "Well Did You Evah?," which was ignored until revived and revised in the 1955 movie *High Society*, and the one substantial hit, "Friendship," a knockabout comic duet for Ethel Merman and Bert Lahr. December 25 brought the insignificant revue, *Folies Bergère*.

In short, it was rather a dismal year for songs on Broadway. As for movies, almost every film historian agrees that 1939 was Hollywood's most brilliant year. It was the year of *Gone with the Wind, The Wizard of Oz, Goodbye, Mr. Chips, Mr. Smith Goes to Washington, Wuthering Heights, Dark Victory, The Women, Juarez, Stanley and Livingstone, The Rains Came, Stagecoach, The Old Maid, Babes in Arms, Confessions of a Nazi Spy, Intermezzo, Jesse James, Gunga Din, The Adventures of Sherlock Holmes, Destry Rides Again, Drums along the Mohawk, Golden Boy, The Hound of the Baskervilles, The Hunchback of Notre Dame, Of Mice and Men, The Story of Vernon and Irene Castle, You Can't Cheat an*

Honest Man, and the list goes on, seemingly forever.

One would expect that with such a flood of cinematic treasures, Hollywood would have provided the public with dozens of top-quality songs. Not so. Using even the most generous definition of a good song, the films of 1939 provided fewer than a dozen!

Certainly the best came from the pens of Harold Arlen and E.Y. "Yip" Harburg. *The Wizard of Oz* gave us the Oscar-winning "Over the Rainbow," memorably sung by young Judy Garland, in addition to "We're Off To See the Wizard" and "If I Only Had a Brain." Arlen and Harburg also gave Groucho Marx one of his classics, "Lydia, the Tattooed Lady," in *At the Circus*.

Also at M-G-M, the studio's resident hit-makers, Arthur Freed and Nacio Herb Brown, gave Judy and Mickey Rooney "Good Morning" for the film version of *Babes in Arms*.

Over at Paramount, Burton Lane and Frank Loesser penned the jaunty "The Lady's in Love with You" for Bob Hope and Shirley Ross to warble in *Some Like It Hot*. The studio also released the Max Fleischer animated feature *Gulliver's Travels* with its attractive "Faithful Forever," written by Leo Robin and Ralph Rainger, and sung by Jessica Dragonette and Lanny Ross.

Three other studios each offered one song hit apiece. The most enduring, "Wishing," by B.G. DeSylva, was introduced by a group of children in RKO's *Love Affair*. Frank Loesser and Frederick Hollander gave Marlene Dietrich her biggest Hollywood hit with "The Boys in the Backroom" in Universal's delightful western *Destry Rides Again*. Despite the usual high standard for songs at 20th Century-Fox, only Irving Berlin's "I Poured My Heart into a Song" from *Second Fiddle* could be considered a success.

Imagine! Only ten important songs from Hollywood in the finest year of its entire history.

If the hit songs of 1939 were not coming from Broadway or Hollywood, where were they coming from? Surprisingly, many of them originated with the classics.

In 1938, band leader Larry Clinton adapted Claude Debussy's piano piece "Reverie" into a sweet, up-to-date ballad called "My Reverie." His recording, with a charming vocal by Bea Wain, was one of the runaway best-selling discs of that year.

Tin Pan Alley, never at a loss for imitating success, began the world's first recycling drive. More than a dozen 1939 songs, many of them highly successful at the time, were based on earlier melodies.

The sadly underrated, highly versatile, and graciously literate Mitchell Parish seemed to have cornered the market on adding lyrics to already existing tunes. His most enduring 1939 hit was certainly "Moonlight Serenade," which is still played as Glenn Miller's theme song. With music by Miller, the song had had an earlier set of words by Edward Heyman under the title "Now I Lay Me down To Sleep." Parish also added lyrics to several Peter De Rose piano pieces, "Deep Purple," "Lilacs in the Rain," and "The Lamp Is Low," the last having been adapted by De Rose and Bert Shefter from Ravel's "Pavane pour une Infante Défunte." Parish also penned the words to "Stairway to the Stars," based on Matt Malneck and Frank Signorelli's "Park Avenue Fantasy."

Over the years, Tchaikovsky posthumously provided more melodies for popular songs than any other concert composer. In 1939, he unwittingly offered themes from *Romeo and Juliet* and the second movement of his fifth symphony. The first was transformed into "Our Love" and recorded by Larry Clinton; and the second became "Moon Love," as arranged by Andre Kostelanetz.

Al Dubin added lyrics to Victor Herbert's 1919 piano piece, "Indian Summer." Lew Sherwood helped

Eddie Duchin fashion his theme song, "My Twilight Dream," from Chopin's Nocturne in E-Flat. Raymond Scott tinkered with Mozart's Sonata in C, and out came "In an Eighteenth Century Drawing Room." Benny Goodman had a hit with "And the Angels Sing," adapted by Johnny Mercer and Ziggy Elman from an old Yiddish song.

There were a few original songs of merit. Bob Crosby's band featured "Day In-Day Out" (Johnny Mercer - Rube Bloom). Woody Herman played his own "Woodchopper's Ball." Hal Kemp had the novelty tune, "Three Little Fishies" by Saxie Dowell. Jimmie Lunceford played Sy Oliver and Trummy Young's "'Taint What You Do (It's the Way That Cha Do It)." And Gene Krupa (with Tiny Parham) wrote his own theme song, "Drummin' Man," as did Cab Calloway with "Jumpin' Jive" and Frankie Masters with "Scatter-Brain."

Among the more romantic songs, 1939 gave us "I'll Never Smile Again" (Ruth Lowe); "If I Didn't Care" (Jack Lawrence), sung to immortality by The Ink Spots; and "I Get Along without You Very Well," with music by Hoagy Carmichael and words from a poem by Mrs. Jane Brown Thompson.

The tensions in Europe gave rise to two patriotic classics. On Armistice Day, 1938, Kate Smith introduced Irving Berlin's stirring "God Bless America," which swept the country the following year. For a time, Smith had exclusive radio rights to the song and performed it week after week on her CBS program, until there was serious discussion about proclaiming it America's national anthem. Also in 1939, Robert Crawford wrote words and music to the official song of the United States Army Air Corps, with its thrilling opening, "Off we go into the wild blue yonder...."

Over in Flushing Meadow, Queens, several songs were introduced at the World's Fair. The theme song of the great event was "Dawn of a New Day," with lyrics by Ira Gershwin and music constructed by Ira and Kay Swift from several tunes left in his trunk by the late George Gershwin. William Grant Still's choral piece, "Song of the City," was performed in the Perisphere, the Fair's theme pavilion. For the *Aquacade*, producer Billy Rose and Ted Fetter wrote words to Dana Suesse melodies, the most popular of which was "Yours for a Song."

The largest building at the Fair housed a spectacular history of railroading in America. During the show, entitled *Railroads on Parade*, authentic trains from the early nineteenth century to modern times rolled out on tracks before an enthralled audience, all to the music of Kurt Weill. One of his themes was transformed into the song "Mile after Mile," with lyrics by Charles Alan (the pageant's director) and Buddy Bernier.

How can one assess the popular songs of 1939? Certainly there were more songs of quality in that one year than America has produced in the last thirty-five years of rock cacophony, but, compared with any year from 1925 to 1935, the quantity is far fewer and quality far lower. However, any year that could turn out "All the Things You Are" and "Over the Rainbow" can't be all bad.

It was the year of the Fair, and a Fair year for songs.

CONTRIBUTORS

JONATHAN SHEFFER IS A COMPOSER AND CONDUCTOR AND THE ARTISTIC DIRECTOR OF EOS MUSIC INC.

ROBERT ROSENBLUM IS PROFESSOR OF FINE ARTS AT THE NEW YORK UNIVERSITY AND PART-TIME CURATOR AT THE GUGGENHEIM MUSEUM.

PIANIST AND MUSICOLOGIST HOWARD POLLACK IS ASSOCIATE PROFESSOR OF MUSIC AT THE UNIVERSITY OF HOUSTON AND THE AUTHOR OF FOUR BOOKS. HIS CRITICAL BIOGRAPHY OF AARON COPLAND IS TO BE PUBLISHED BY HENRY HOLT.

JOHN BELL TEACHES THEATER HISTORY AND PRACTICE AT NEW YORK UNIVERSITY AND RHODE ISLAND SCHOOL OF DESIGN. HE IS A MEMBER OF THE GREAT SMALL WORKS THEATER COMPANY AND HAS WORKED WITH BREAD AND PUPPET THEATER SINCE 1973.

ROSEMARIE HAAG BLETTER IS PROFESSOR OF ARCHITECTURAL HISTORY AT THE GRADUATE CENTER, CITY UNIVERSITY OF NEW YORK. SHE HAS WRITTEN ON CONTEMPORARY AMERICAN ARCHITECTURE AS WELL AS GERMAN EXPRESSIONISM AND OTHER MODERNISMS OF THE 1920S.

MILES KREUGER IS THE PRESIDENT OF THE INSTITUTE OF THE AMERICAN MUSICAL IN LOS ANGELES AND THE AUTHOR OF *SHOW BOAT: THE STORY OF A CLASSIC AMERICAN MUSICAL* AND HUNDREDS OF ARTICLES ON MUSICAL THEATRE AND FILM.

CLAUDIA SWAN IS AN ASSISTANT PROFESSOR OF ART HISTORY AT THE PENNSYLVANIA STATE UNIVERSITY.

CREDITS

I M A G E S : View of the Fair Grounds, New York World's Fair 1939-40 Records, Manuscripts and Archives Division, The New York Public Library, Astor, Lenox and Tilden Foundations; Trylon and Perisphere with Sculptures and Lake, New York World's Fair 1939-40 Records, Manuscripts and Archives Division, The New York Public Library, Astor, Lenox and Tilden Foundations; Artist's Rendering of Democracity, New York World's Fair 1939-40 Records, Manuscripts and Archives Division, The New York Public Library, Astor, Lenox and Tilden Foundations; Piano Festival at the Court of Peace, New York World's Fair 1939-40 Records, Manuscripts and Archives Division, The New York Public Library, Astor, Lenox and Tilden Foundations; Trylon and Perisphere under Construction, New York World's Fair 1939-40 Records, Manuscripts and Archives Division, The New York Public

Library, Astor, Lenox and Tilden Foundations; Hall of Pharmacy, Architect's Rendering, New York World's Fair 1939-40 Records, Manuscripts and Archives Division, The New York Public Library, Astor, Lenox and Tilden Foundations; Rudy Burckhardt, Photograph of William de Kooning, Sketch for Hall of Pharmacy Mural, Courtesy Tibor de Nagy Gallery, New York; Portrait of Aaron Copland, Music Division, Lincoln Center for the Performing Arts, The New York Public Library, Astor, Lenox and Tilden Foundations; Remo Bufano and his Witch, The Alchemist with Child, and Bufano and his Witch Doctor, from *Life Magazine* May 1, 1939, General Research Division, The New York Public Library, Astor, Lenox and Tilden Foundations; Remo Bufano and Assistant at Work on Witch Puppet, New York World's Fair 1939-40 Records, Manuscripts and Archives Division, The New York Public Library, Astor, Lenox and Tilden Foundations; **P L A T E I** General Plan of Fair Grounds, Wall Mural, 15 x 20 ft, in America Art Today Pavilion, New York World's Fair 1939-40 Records, Manuscripts and Archives Division, The New York Public Library, Astor, Lenox and Tilden Foundations; **P L A T E II** Marching Band, New York World's Fair 1939-40 Records, Manuscripts and Archives Division, The New York Public Library, Astor, Lenox and Tilden Foundations; **P L A T E III** Food Focal Exhibit – Man, New York World's Fair 1939-40 Records, Manuscripts and Archives Division, The New York Public Library, Astor, Lenox and Tilden Foundations; **P L A T E IV** Elektro, Westinghouse Moto-Man, New York World's Fair 1939-40 Records, Manuscripts and Archives Division, The New York Public Library, Astor, Lenox and Tilden Foundations; **P L A T E V** Billy Rose's Aquacade, New York World's Fair 1939-40 Records, Manuscripts and Archives Division, The New York Public Library, Astor, Lenox and Tilden Foundations; **P L A T E VI** Stereo View: Illuminated Fountains., Lagoon of Nations, at Night (Rogers and Rogers), Photography Collection, Miriam and Ira D. Wallach Division of Art, Prints and Photographs, The New York Public Library, Astor, Lenox and Tilden Foundations; **P L A T E VII** Concert Hall, Architect's Rendering, New York World's Fair 1939-40 Records, Manuscripts and Archives Division, The New York Public Library, Astor, Lenox and Tilden Foundations; **P L A T E VIII** Ferde Grofé, Composer and Conductor, Leads his Children in a Nursery Rhyme at America at Home Exhibit, New York World's Fair 1939-40 Records, Manuscripts and Archives Division, The New York Public Library, Astor, Lenox and Tilden Foundations; **P L A T E IX** Portrait of William Grant Still, New York World's Fair 1939-40 Records, Manuscripts and Archives Division, The New York Public Library, Astor, Lenox and Tilden Foundations; **P L A T E X** Electrical Products Building, New York World's Fair 1939-40 Records, Manuscripts and Archives Division, The New York Public Library, Astor, Lenox and Tilden Foundations; **P L A T E XI** The "Elmer" Poster, New York World's Fair 1939-40 Records, Manuscripts and Archives Division, The New York Public Library, Astor, Lenox and Tilden Foundations; **P L A T E XII** Theme Center, Viewed from Ramp, New York World's Fair 1939-40 Records, Manuscripts and Archives Division, The New York Public Library, Astor, Lenox and Tilden Foundations; Film Still from *The City* (Traffic Jam on NYC street), Film Stills Archive, The Museum of Modern Art, New York; Ford Exhibit: Crowd Listening to "Roll Over" Chassis Lecture, New York World's Fair 1939-40 Records, Manuscripts and Archives Division, The New York Public Library, Astor, Lenox and Tilden Foundations; Louis Prima Knocking out a Hot Note, New York World's Fair 1939-40 Records, Manuscripts and Archives Division, The New York Public Library, Astor, Lenox and Tilden Foundations; Rockettes on Outdoor Stage, New York World's Fair 1939-40 Records, Manuscripts and Archives Division, The New York Public Library, Astor, Lenox and Tilden Foundations; Aerial View of the Fair Grounds, with Manhattan Skyline in the Background, New York World's Fair 1939-40 Records, Manuscripts and Archives Division, The New York Public Library, Astor, Lenox and Tilden Foundations.

PHOTO RESEARCH BY ELIZABETH A. WYCKOFF

T E X T S : Art at the New York World's Fair ©1998 Robert Rosenblum; Copland at the Fair ©1998 Howard Pollack; From Sorcery to Science ©1998 John Bell; Architectural Modernisms ©1998 Rosemarie Haag Bletter; 1939: A Fair Year for Popular Songs ©1998 Miles Kreuger